Best Chicken Wing Ideas

Quick Chicken Wing Recipes, Best Hot Wings Recipe, Fried Chicken, And A Complete Cookbook Of Wing Ideas!

Copyright © 2021 Wizard Chef

All rights reserved. No part of this publication may be reproduced, stored in or introduced into a retrieval system, or transmitted, in any form, or by any means (electronic, mechanical, photocopying, recording, or otherwise) without the prior written permission of the copyright owner of this book and is illegal and punishable by law.

Although the author and publisher have made every effort to ensure that the information in this book was correct at press time, the author and publisher do not assume and hereby disclaim any liability to any party for any loss, damage, or disruption caused by errors or omissions, whether such errors or omissions result from negligence, accident, or any other cause. The views expressed are those of the author alone, and should not be taken as expert instruction or commands. The reader is responsible for his or her own actions.

Neither the author nor the publisher assumes any responsibility or liability whatsoever on the behalf of the purchaser or reader of these materials. Any perceived slight of any individual or organization is purely unintentional.

DOWNLOAD Your Free Gift Now!

As a way of saying "thank you" for your purchase, I'm going to share with you a **Free Gift** that is exclusive to readers of "300 Chicken Recipes". This will help you to prepare your dishes easily and effortlessly without hassle!

Click Here to Check it Out

Or visit:

https://www.wizard-chef.com/wizardchefmaster

Table Of Contents

Introduction 6

History of Chicken & Buffalo Wings 6

Chicken Wings and Football Liaison 6

Deep-fried Chicken Wings.. 7

Famous Chicken Wings All Over the World 8

Buffalo Wing Trivia 9

C O O K B O O K 10

   1. GARLIC PIRI-PIRI CHICKEN WINGS 10

   2. Baked Buffalo Wings with Spicy Sauce 12

   3. Chicken Wings in Soy-Garlic-Honey Marinade 14

   4. 'Superfreak' Hot Wings... 16

   5. Parmesan Chicken Wings 18

   6. Chicken Wings in Hot Honey Sauce 20

   7. Chicken Wings in Sherry - Oyster Sauce 22

   8. Tabasco Chicken Wings in Peanut Butter 24

   9. Express Super-Hot Chicken Wings 26

   10. Piquant Chicken Wings in BBQ Sauce 28

   11. Grilled Orange-Honey Chicken Wings 30

   12. Chicken Wings in Hot Mustard Sauce 32

   13. Chicken Wings in Balsamic-Basil Sauce (Slow Cooker) ... 34

   14. Hot Wings with Turmeric - Garlic Marinade.................... 36

   15. Chicken Wings in Black Wine Marinade.......................... 38

   16. Savory Chicken Wings (Microwave)................................. 40

   17. Glazed Chicken Wings (Chinese style).............................42

18. Instant Pot Buffalo Wings 44

19. Chicken Wings with Spicy Rosemary 46

20. "Beery" Chicken Wings (grill) 48

21. Pepper Jack Hot Wings (oven) 50

22. Teriyaki Style Chicken Wings 52

23. Smoked BBQ Chicken Wings 54

24. Japanese Spicy Chicken Wings 56

25. Air Fryer Chicken Wings in Tamari Marinade 58

26. Lemon Pepper Wings in Crockpot 60

27. Crispy Breaded Chicken Wings 62

28. Mexican Hot Chicken Wings 64

29. Chicken Wings with Darker Maple Syrup Glaze 66

30. Buffalo Wild Hot Sauce Wings 68

Summary 70

Sources 71

Congrats! Note from the Wizard Chef 72

Introduction

History of Chicken & Buffalo Wings

They say all great ideas are discovered simultaneously across the world. For chicken & Buffalo wings, that must have meant a simultaneous lip smack that was so loud that it was heard worldwide. Officially, the invention is claimed by a Buffalo, New York bar owner that wanted to use leftover chicken wings for a late-night snack fiesta sometime in 1964.

Fast food chains adopted the wings during the 90s who gave their twist to the recipe but always kept the spiciness. This turned out to be a splendid combination with beer during football season, ramping up the excitement in bars. Groups of fans would gather around a pile of chicken wings, relating and sharing the experience.

Chicken Wings and Football Liaison

Bars that wanted to offer their patrons something more substantial realized the chicken wings are the perfect upgrade to peanuts and similar snacks. The spiciness and saltiness promoted thirst in patrons, which in turn meant more drinks sold. Besides, the chicken wings were dirt cheap, rich in protein, and had a real crunch.

Chicken wings are also easy to eat without looking at them, perfect for sports matches where every second matter. With the advent of satellite TV and regular football matches, people gathered in bars to cheer their team and munch on the new favorite snack of the whole world — Buffalo wings.

Deep-fried Chicken Wings

Though deep-fried chicken wings were discovered by accident, closer examination shows that's not the case. Chicken wings were the least favorite part of the chicken during meat processing, seeing how consumers preferred drumsticks and chicken breasts. This created an excess of perfectly edible, albeit unsightly, chicken parts usually tossed away as refuse or sold for pennies to impoverished families to be used in soups. Another favorable attribute of chicken wings is that they absorb all kinds of flavors.

The Original Recipe

An interesting detail is that the original recipe of Buffalo wings included celery sticks, which are served to this day alongside Buffalo wings. However, in posh restaurants, they might take the form of cubes. One explanation is that their excellent, refreshing taste offsets the spiciness and cleans that palate for the next round of chicken wings. Another traditional addition to Buffalo wings is the blue cheese dip. When looked at as a whole, now it makes sense whey the celery sticks — they are consumable cutlery so that each eater can dip into the cheese without making a mess. Some eaters will replace the cheese dip with Ranch dressing, though the hardcore Buffalo wing fans consider a watered-down version of the original recipe.

Famous Chicken Wings All Over the World

There are so many ways to prepare delicious chicken wings.

Thai coconut yellow curry chicken, hot Mexican style, Asian soy and tamari style, tandoori chicken, chicken with honey, garlic, hot sauce, lemon-pepper, sweet chili, Honey BBQ, Buffalo sauce, chicken wings baked in the oven, grilled, or deep-fried, we have delicious, simple chicken recipes to help you get back for more.

No matter how you prepare the wings, you will not go wrong, generally, provided that your home loves them because the principle of preparation is mostly the same. Everything else is your creative cooking inspiration.

Buffalo Wing Trivia

The National Buffalo Wing Day has been celebrated in Buffalo, New York, each July 29, starting from 1993. In just a few days, the 100,000-strong attendees will eat up to 30 tons of chicken wings, with some of them being genuine competitive eaters. In 2008, Joey Chestnut managed to down 241 Buffalo wings in 28 minutes, setting the festival record, though he did get a break at the mid-way point.

The next generation of competitive eaters took a liking to Buffalo wings, with Patrick Bertoletti managing to send a whopping 444 Buffalo wings down his chute in 2015.

COOKBOOK

1. GARLIC PIRI-PIRI CHICKEN WINGS

Servings: 4   **Preparation Time:** 55 minutes

Nutrition Facts: Serving size: 1/4 of a recipe (8 ounces)

Percent daily values based on the Reference Daily Intake (RDI) for a 2000 calorie diet.

(Calories 550, Total Fat 44, Total Carbohydrates 18g, Sugar 12g Protein 24g)

Ingredients

Crushed garlic cloves (about 8)

1 cup of vegetable oil (Canola or peanut)

Salt to taste

3 1/2 lbs. chicken wings

1/3 cup of fresh lemon juice

1 scoop of wheat flour

2 Tbsp crushed chiles

1/3 cup of corn flour

1 Tbsp apple cider vinegar

1/3 cup of cornstarch

Instructions

1. Mix the garlic, salt, lemon juice, chiles, vinegar, and 1/3 cup of oil in a bowl; stir to combine well.

2. Place the wings in a large container; pour the garlic mixture evenly over the chicken and toss to combine well.

3. Refrigerate them overnight.

4. Remove the chicken wings from the marinade and roll each piece into a flour mixture.

5. Heat oil in a large non-stick saucepan over medium-high heat (to 375 degrees).

6. Fry your chicken wings for about 4 minutes per side or until crispy.

7. Drain your chicken wings on a wire rack or onto kitchen paper.

8. Serve warm.

2. Baked Buffalo Wings with Spicy Sauce

Servings: 4   **Preparation Time:** 55 to 60 minutes

Nutrition Facts: Serving size: 1/4 of a recipe (8 ounces)

Percent daily values based on the Reference Daily Intake (RDI) for a 2000 calorie diet.

(Calories 564, Total Fat 4422, Total Carbohydrates 14g, Sugar 12g Protein 22g)

Ingredients

3 pounds of chicken wings (about 14 to 16)

1/2 cup of vegetable oil (canola, peanut)

1 cup Hot red sauce (any)

3 Tbsp butter melted

1 tsp cumin

1 tsp cayenne pepper (optional)

Salt to taste

Instructions

1. Preheat oven to 450 F.

2. Place the chicken wings in a large container and season with salt.

3. In a separate bowl, mix all remaining ingredients and pour the mixture over the chicken.

4. Arrange the chicken wings in a large baking dish or sheet along with the sauce.

5. Bake for about 50 minutes or until internal temperature reaches 165°F.

6. Remove from the oven and serve warm.

3. Chicken Wings in Soy-Garlic-Honey Marinade

Servings: 4   **Preparation Time**: 55 minutes

Nutrition Facts: Serving size: 1/4 of a recipe (8 ounces)

Percent daily values based on the Reference Daily Intake (RDI) for a 2000 calorie diet.

(Calories 402.12, Total Fat 22, Total Carbohydrates 28g, Sugar 22g Protein 21g)

Ingredients

1/2 cup of soy sauce   5 clove garlic, minced

2 Tbsp of sesame oil   1 grated onion

4 Tbsp honey

1 Tbsp of red pepper paste

2 Tbsp granulated sugar

2 lbs. chicken wings

1 tsp of fresh ginger, grated

Instructions

1. Mix all ingredients in a large container (except chicken wings).

2. Add chicken wings and cover with the mixture.

3. Marinate the chicken overnight.

4. Preheat oven to 400 F.

5. Transfer chicken wings and drumsticks onto a large baking pan along with the marinade.

6. Bake for about 40 to 50 minutes, turning once during cooking.

7. Remove chicken wings from the oven.

8. Serve warm.

4. 'Superfreak' Hot Wings

Servings: 4

Preparation Time: 1 hour and 10 minutes

Nutrition Facts: Serving size: 1/4 of a recipe (8 ounces)

Percent daily values based on the Reference Daily Intake (RDI) for a 2000 calorie diet.

(Calories 503, Total Fat 20, Total Carbohydrates 18g, Sugar 16g Protein 22g)

Ingredients

Sauce

1 Tbsp baking powder

3/4 cup of hot sauce

1/4 cup of butter melted

1 tsp sea salt

2 tsp crushed red paprika (or to taste)

2 Tbsp Worcestershire sauce

4 lbs. chicken wings

Instructions

1. Preheat oven to 400 F.

2. Line a large baking sheet with foil.

3. Mix all ingredients for the sauce in a large bowl.

4. Brush every chicken wing with the sauce and place it onto a baking sheet.

5. Pour any leftover sauce over the chicken.

6. Bake for 50 to 55 minutes.

7. Serve immediately.

5. Parmesan Chicken Wings

Servings: 4

Preparation Time: 1 hour

Nutrition Facts: Serving size: 1/4 of a recipe (8 ounces)

Percent daily values based on the Reference Daily Intake (RDI) for a 2000 calorie diet.

(Calories 421, Total Fat 42, Total Carbohydrates 10g, Sugar 2g Protein 31g)

Ingredients

4 lbs. chicken wings

Salt and ground pepper to taste

1/3 cup of melted butter

1 cup of grated Parmesan

3/4 cup of breadcrumbs

1/2 cup of fresh cream

Fresh parsley for serving (optional)

Instructions

1. Preheat oven to 380 F.

2. Season the chicken wings with salt and pepper.

3. Arrange the chicken onto a large, greased baking sheet.

4. Mix the butter, parmesan, breadcrumbs, and cream in a bowl.

5. Sprinkle the mixture evenly over the chicken wings.

6. Bake for about 45 to 50 minutes or until a thermometer inserted in the chicken reaches 165 degrees F.

7. Sprinkle with chopped parsley and serve warm.

6. Chicken Wings in Hot Honey Sauce

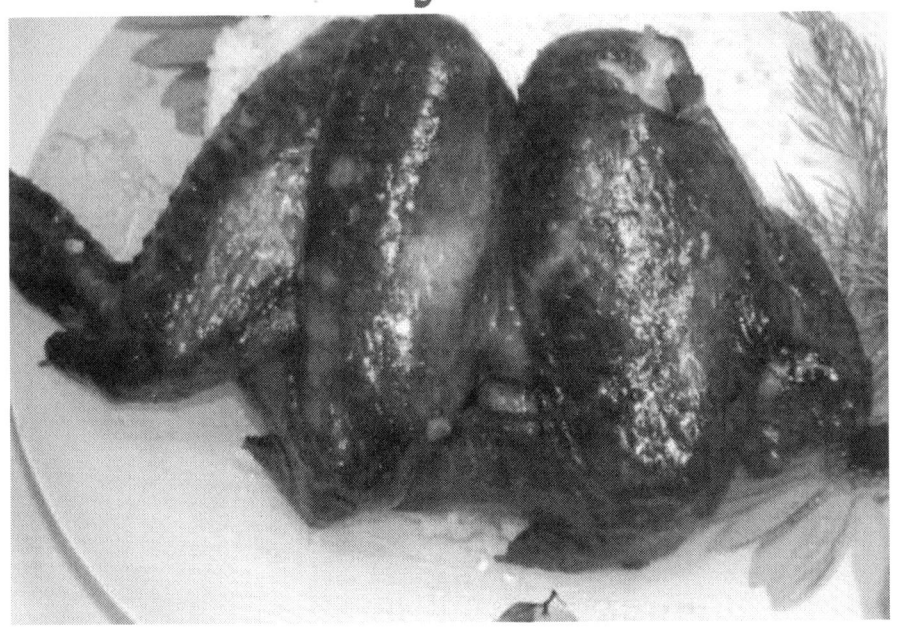

Servings: 4   **Preparation Time**: 1 hour

Nutrition Facts: Serving size: 1/4 of a recipe (8 ounces)

Percent daily values based on the Reference Daily Intake (RDI) for a 2000 calorie diet.

(Calories 421, Total Fat 27, Total Carbohydrates 19g, Sugar 12g Protein 33g)

Ingredients

18 to 20 chicken wings

Salt to taste

4 cloves garlic minced

3 Tbsp strained honey

1/3 cup of melted butter

4 Tbsp hot sauce

Instructions

1. Season the chicken wings with salt.

2. Place the chicken into a large container.

3. Mix all remaining ingredients and pour over chicken.

4. Refrigerate for at least two hours.

5. Preheat oven to 380 F.

6. Place the chicken onto a large, greased baking sheet along with its juices.

7. Bake for about 45 to 50 minutes.

8. Serve warm.

7. Chicken Wings in Sherry - Oyster Sauce

Servings: 4   **Preparation Time:** 55 minutes

Nutrition Facts: Serving size: 1/4 of a recipe (8 ounces)

Percent daily values based on the Reference Daily Intake (RDI) for a 2000 calorie diet.

(Calories 414, Total Fat 20, Total Carbohydrates 33g, Sugar 25g Protein 21g)

Ingredients

Marinade

4 Tbsp oyster sauce   3 Tbsp dry sherry

4 Tbsp soy sauce   2 Tbsp water

2 Tbsp rice oil   1 shallot finely diced

2 cloves mince garlic   salt and pepper to taste

Chicken

4 lbs. chicken wings (about 15 to 18)

Instructions

1. Mix all ingredients for the marinade in a large container.

2. Add the chicken wings and toss to cover well.

3. Refrigerate for two hours or overnight.

4. Preheat oven to 400 F.

5. Place the chicken wings along with the marinade in a large baking dish.

6. Bake for about 50 to 55 minutes.

7. Serve hot.

8. Tabasco Chicken Wings in Peanut Butter

Servings: 4   **Preparation Time:** 55 minutes

Nutrition Facts: Serving size: 1/4 of a recipe (8 ounces)

Percent daily values based on the Reference Daily Intake (RDI) for a 2000 calorie diet.

(Calories 525, Total Fat 30, Total Carbohydrates 32g, Sugar 18g Protein 22g)

Ingredients

1/3 cup of peanut butter

4 oz fresh butter softened

4 Tbsp Tabasco sauce

Salt and white pepper to taste

Pinch of cayenne pepper

4 lbs. chicken wings (18 to 20)

Instructions

1. Preheat oven to 400 F.

2. Brush generously two large baking sheets with the peanut butter; set aside.

3. Heat the butter, Tabasco, salt, pepper, and cayenne in a saucepan until boil; remove from the heat.

4. Place the chicken wings on a container and cover with butter-Tabasco sauce; mix well.

5. Place the chicken onto prepared baking sheets.

6. Bake for 50 to 55 minutes.

7. Serve warm.

9. Express Super-Hot Chicken Wings

Servings: 4   **Preparation Time:** 25 to 30 minutes

Nutrition Facts: Serving size: 1/4 of a recipe (8 ounces)

Percent daily values based on the Reference Daily Intake (RDI) for a 2000 calorie diet.

(Calories 487, Total Fat 26, Total Carbohydrates 21g, Sugar 18g Protein 22g)

Ingredients

Marinade

1/3 cup of butter softened

1 Tbsp brown sugar

2 Tbsp tomato paste

2 cloves of garlic crushed

1 Tbsp tamari sauce

2 tsp cayenne pepper

1 Tbsp Harissa or red chili paste

20 chicken wings cleaned

1 cup water for Instant pot

Salt to taste

Instructions

1. Mix all marinade ingredients in a saucepan over medium heat.

2. Bring to boil and remove from the heat; set aside to cool down.

3. Place the chicken wings in a large container and cover them evenly with the marinade.

4. Cover, toss and refrigerate for at least 4 hours.

5. Pour one cup of water into Instant Pot and place the trivet.

6. Arrange few chicken wings onto the trivet.

7. Lock lid into place and set on the MANUAL setting high pressure for 5 minutes.

8. When the beep sounds, flip the Quick Release valve to let the pressure out.

9. Repeat the process as many times as needed.

10. Serve warm.

10. Piquant Chicken Wings in BBQ Sauce

Servings: 4

Preparation Time: 55 minutes

Nutrition Facts: Serving size: 1/4 of a recipe (8 ounces)

Percent daily values based on the Reference Daily Intake (RDI) for a 2000 calorie diet.

(Calories 484, Total Fat 24, Total Carbohydrates 28g, Sugar 18g Protein 21g)

Ingredients

Marinade

1 1/2 cups of BBQ sauce

3 Tbsp honey

2 tsp Tabasco sauce

2 tsp Worcestershire sauces

2 tsp hot mustard

Salt and pepper to taste

28

3 to 4 lbs. chicken wings (15 to 20 pieces)

Instructions

1. Mix all marinade ingredients in a saucepan.

2. Heat the mixture over medium heat.

3. Bring to boil and remove from the heat.

4. Preheat oven to 400 G.

5. Place the chicken wings into a large container and cover with the BBQ sauce.

6. Place the chicken wings along with sauce onto a large, greased baking sheet.

7. Bake for about 50 to 55 minutes.

8. Serve warm.

11. Grilled Orange-Honey Chicken Wings

Servings: 4   **Preparation Time:** 55 to 60 minutes

Nutrition Facts: Serving size: 1/4 of a recipe (8 ounces)

Percent daily values based on the Reference Daily Intake (RDI) for a 2000 calorie diet.

(Calories 564, Total Fat 22, Total Carbohydrates 14g, Sugar 12g Protein 22g)

Ingredients

2 Tbsp mustard (any)

2 Tbsp honey strained

1/2 cup of fresh orange juice

Salt and ground red pepper to taste

3 lbs. chicken wings

Instructions

1. In a bowl, mix the mustard, honey, orange juice, salt, and red pepper; stir to combine well.

2. Place the chicken wings onto the large sheet and brush generously with the mixture; let them sit for 15 minutes.

3. Oil the grill racks and preheat your grill (any) to a high temperature.

4. Arrange your chicken wings onto grill racks, close the lid and cook for 10 minutes.

5. Open the lid and turn around the chicken.

6. Close the lid and cook for a further ten minutes.

7. Open the lid and check the internal chicken temperature.

8. Your chicken wings are ready when all of them reach 165ºF.

9. Serve warm.

12. Chicken Wings in Hot Mustard Sauce

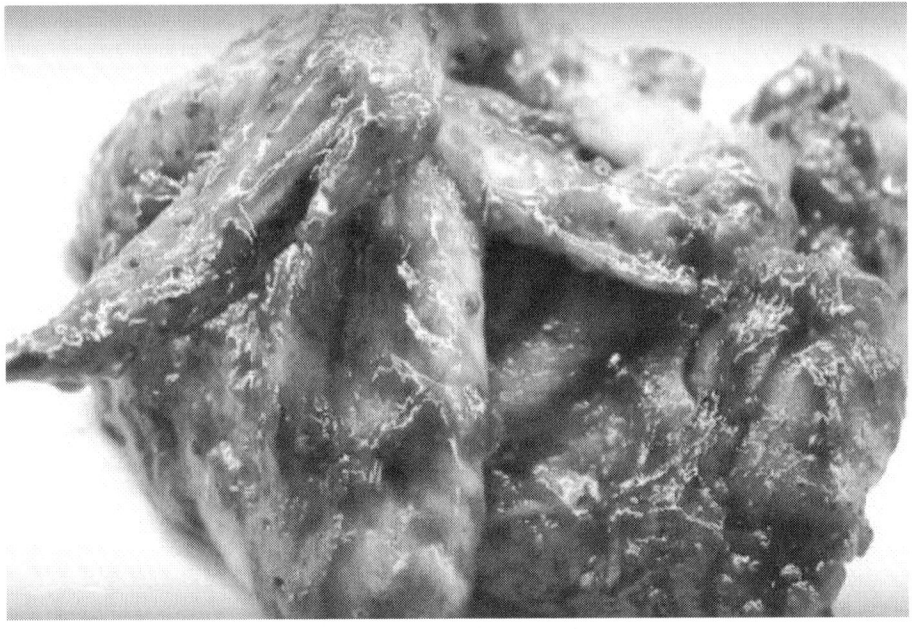

Servings: 4

Preparation Time: 1 hour and 10 minutes

Nutrition Facts:

Serving size: 1/4 of a recipe (8 ounces)

Percent daily values based on the Reference Daily Intake (RDI) for a 2000 calorie diet.

(Calories 503, Total Fat 20, Total Carbohydrates 18g, Sugar 16g Protein 22g)

Ingredients

3 lbs. chicken wings cleaned

Marinade

2 Tbsp olive oil

3 tsp garlic powder

Fresh lemon juice of 2 lemons

2 Tbsp mustard

3 Tbsp hot ketchup

1 Tbsp Tabasco sauce

1 tsp fresh thyme

1 tsp ground cayenne pepper

2 Tbsp brown sugar

Salt to taste

Instructions

1. Place the chicken wings in a large container.

2. Mix well all ingredients for the sauce.

3. Pour the mixture over chicken wings and marinate in refrigerate overnight.

4. Preheat oven to 350 F.

5. Line a large baking sheet with foil and arrange the chicken wings.

6. Bake for 55 to 60 minutes.

7. Serve hot.

13. Chicken Wings in Balsamic-Basil Sauce (Slow Cooker)

Servings: 4

Preparation Time: 4 hours and 10 minutes

Nutrition Facts: Serving size: 1/4 of a recipe (8 ounces)

Percent daily values based on the Reference Daily Intake (RDI) for a 2000 calorie diet.

(Calories 478, Total Fat 18, Total Carbohydrates 14g, Sugar 11g Protein 22g)

Ingredients

20 chicken wings

Salt and freshly ground black pepper to taste

Sauce

3 Tbsp vegetable oil

1/2 cup of red wine

4 Tbsp balsamic vinegar

2 Tbsp granulated sugar

4 Tbsp water

1 bunch of fresh basil finely chopped

Instructions

1. Season the chicken wings with salt and pepper.

2. Place them on the bottom of the Slow Cooker.

3. Mix all remaining ingredients in a bowl; stir to combine well.

4. Pour the mixture evenly over the chicken wings.

5. Cook on HIGH for 2 hours or on SLOW for 4 hours.

6. Serve warm.

14. Hot Wings with Turmeric - Garlic Marinade

Servings: 4

Preparation Time: 1 hour and 5 minutes

Nutrition Facts:

Serving size: 1/4 of a recipe (8 ounces)

Percent daily values based on the Reference Daily Intake (RDI) for a 2000 calorie diet.

(Calories 488, Total Fat 18, Total Carbohydrates 18g, Sugar 13g Protein 22g)

Ingredients

Marinade

6 cloves garlic minced

2 red chili peppers finely chopped

1 green onion finely chopped

1 tsp turmeric powder

2 Tbsp water

2 Tbsp hot pepper sauce

1 Tbsp brown sugar

4 Tbsp olive oil

salt and red ground pepper to taste

20 chicken wings

Instructions

1. Mix all ingredients in a bowl; stir to combine well.

2. Place the chicken wings onto a large baking sheet and generously brush with marinade.

3. Refrigerate them for at least two hours.

4. Preheat oven to 400 F.

5. Linea large baking sheet with aluminum foil and arrange the chicken wings.

6. Bake for about 50 to 55 minutes.

7. Serve warm.

15. Chicken Wings in Black Wine Marinade

Servings: 4 **Preparation Time:** 55 minutes

Nutrition Facts: Serving size: 1/4 of a recipe (8 ounces)

Percent daily values based on the Reference Daily Intake (RDI) for a 2000 calorie diet.

(Calories 530, Total Fat 34, Total Carbohydrates 33g, Sugar 20g Protein 21g)

Ingredients

4 lbs. Chicken wings

<u>Marinade</u>

1 cup of butter melted   2/3 cup of brown sugar

3/4 cup of red wine   2 tsp dry garlic

Instructions

1. Preheat oven to 400 F.

2. Heat all ingredients for the marinade and bring to boil; remove from the oven.

3. Place the chicken wings into a large container and cover with the marinade.

6. Arrange the chicken wings with sauce onto a greased baking sheet.

7. Bake for about 50 to 55 minutes.

8. Serve warm.

16. Savory Chicken Wings (Microwave)

Servings: 4

Preparation Time: 1 hour and 10 minutes

Nutrition Facts: Serving size: 1/4 of a recipe (8 ounces)

Percent daily values based on the Reference Daily Intake (RDI) for a 2000 calorie diet.

(Calories 421, Total Fat 22, Total Carbohydrates 18g, Sugar 12g Protein 21g)

Ingredients

2 packages of fully cooked chicken wings

Sauce

1/2 cup of buffalo sauce

1/3 cup of melted butter

1/2 tsp ground red pepper   Salt to taste

1 Tbsp apple cider vinegar

Instructions

1. Place 6 chicken wings onto a microwaveable dish with little space between them.

2. Mix all ingredients for the sauce and pour a third of the mixture over the chicken.

3. Cook your chicken in a microwave oven for about 5 to 6 minutes or until they are no longer pink inside.

4. Remove from the microwave and place chicken onto serving plate; cover and set aside.

5. Repeat the process twice (for 18 to 20 chicken wings)

6. Serve.

17. Glazed Chicken Wings (Chinese style)

Servings: 4   **Preparation Time:** 55 to 60 minutes

Nutrition Facts: Serving size: 1/4 of a recipe (8 ounces)

Percent daily values based on the Reference Daily Intake (RDI) for a 2000 calorie diet.

(Calories 512, Total Fat 24, Total Carbohydrates 19g, Sugar 13g Protein 21g)

Ingredients

Marinade

1/2 cup of soy sauce

1/4 cup of dry white wine

4 Tbsp soybean oil (canola or avocado oil)

1/4 tsp cinnamon

1/4 tsp fennel seeds

18 to 20 chicken wings

Fresh ground black pepper to taste

Instructions

1. Mix all marinade ingredients in a large plastic bag.

2. Add the chicken wings and toss to combine well.

3. Refrigerate it for about four hours (or overnight).

4. Preheat oven to 400 F.

5. Drain the chicken and arrange it onto a large baking sheet.

6. Bake for about 35 to 45 minutes.

7. Serve warm.

18. Instant Pot Buffalo Wings

Servings: 4

Preparation Time: 25 to 30 minutes

Nutrition Facts:

Serving size: 1/4 of a recipe (8 ounces)

Percent daily values based on the Reference Daily Intake (RDI) for a 2000 calorie diet.

(Calories 520, Total Fat 28, Total Carbohydrates 18g, Sugar 13g Protein 22g)

Ingredients

Marinade

1/2 cup of hot sauce

2 Tbsp Maple syrup

1 Tbsp apple cider vinegar

Pinch of cinnamon

1/4 cup of melted butter

1 Tbsp crushed pepper

Salt and ground pepper to taste

20 chicken wings

1 cup water for Instant pot

Instructions

1. Mix all marinade ingredients in a bowl.

2. Place the chicken wings in a large container and cover evenly with the marinade; toss to combine well.

3. Refrigerate them for at least 4 hours or overnight.

4. Pour the water into your Instant pot and place the trivet inside.

5. Place the wings on the top of the trivet.

6. Lock lid into place and set on the MANUAL setting high pressure for 5 minutes.

7. When the timer beeps, press "Cancel" and use the Quick release.

8. Repeat the same process until you finish with all the chicken wings.

9. Serve warm.

19. Chicken Wings with Spicy Rosemary

Servings: 4

Preparation Time: 1 hour and 10 minutes

Nutrition Facts: Serving size: 1/4 of a recipe (8 ounces)

Percent daily values based on the Reference Daily Intake (RDI) for a 2000 calorie diet.

(Calories 503, Total Fat 20, Total Carbohydrates 18g, Sugar 16g Protein 22g)

Ingredients

20 chicken wings

10 sprigs of rosemary finely chopped

6 cloves garlic minced

4 Tbsp olive oil,

1 tsp crushed hot pepper

Salt to taste

1 Tbsp Tabasco sauce

Instructions

1. Preheat oven to 380 F.

2. Place the chicken wings onto a large, greased baking sheet and season with salt.

3. Mix the rosemary, garlic, olive oil, hot pepper, Tabasco sauce, and salt in a bowl.

4. Generously brush the chicken wings with the mixture.

5. Bake for 45 to 55 minutes.

6. Serve warm.

20. "Beery" Chicken Wings (grill)

Servings: 4

Preparation Time: 1 hour and 5 minutes

Nutrition Facts: Serving size: 1/4 of a recipe (8 ounces)

Percent daily values based on the Reference Daily Intake (RDI) for a 2000 calorie diet.

(Calories 406, Total Fat 16, Total Carbohydrates 17g, Sugar 10g Protein 27g)

Ingredients

20 chicken wings

Marinade

2 Tbsp chicken fat melted

2 cups of beer

1/2 cup barbecue sauce

1 Tbsp soy sauce

1/4 tsp ground red pepper   Salt to taste

1/4 tsp cayenne pepper

Instructions

1. Place the chicken wings in a large container.

2. Mix all ingredients for the marinade in a bowl; stir to combine well.

3. Pour the mixture over the chicken and toss to combine well.

4. Refrigerate for at least 4 hours.

5. Heat the grill to medium-high.

6. Arrange the chicken wings onto grill racks.

7. Cover and cook your chicken for about 10 minutes.

8. Using grill tongs, turn the chicken on the other side.

9. Cook covered for a further 10 minutes.

10. Serve warm.

21. Pepper Jack Hot Wings (oven)

Servings: 4   **Preparation Time:** 1 hour and 10 minutes

Nutrition Facts: Serving size: 1/4 of a recipe (8 ounces)

Percent daily values based on the Reference Daily Intake (RDI) for a 2000 calorie diet.

(Calories 421, Total Fat 22, Total Carbohydrates 18g, Sugar 12g Protein 21g)

Ingredients

18 to 20 chicken wings

Salt and ground pepper to taste

Sauce

1 cup of spicy white sauce (or red)

1 Tbsp Worchester sauce

2 to 3 Tbsp melted butter

1 tsp cayenne pepper

1/2 cup of Pepper Jack cheese crumbled

1 tsp crushed paprika

Instructions

1. Preheat oven to 400 F.

2. Season the chicken wings with salt and pepper; place onto a large, greased baking sheet.

3. Mix all ingredients for the sauce in a bowl; stir to combine well.

4. Pour the sauce over the chicken evenly.

5. Cover with foil and bake for about 30 minutes.

6. Remove the foil and cook for a further 15 to 20 minutes.

7. Serve warm.

Authors note:

You can replace the Pepper Jack cheese with Gouda or Gorgonzola cheese.

22. Teriyaki Style Chicken Wings

Servings: 4   **Preparation Time:** 1 hour

Nutrition Facts: Serving size: 1/4 of a recipe (8 ounces)

Percent daily values based on the Reference Daily Intake (RDI) for a 2000 calorie diet.

(Calories 567, Total Fat 48, Total Carbohydrates 14g, Sugar 6g Protein 37g)

Ingredients

3 lbs. chicken wings

<u>Marinade</u>

1 salt soy sauce   1 cup of water

1/2 cup of honey

1/2 cup of brown sugar

1/4 cup of apple cider vinegar

1/4 cup of rice oil (or avocado)

1 Tbsp crushed garlic

1 tsp ginger powder

Instructions

1. Place the chicken wings in a large container.

2. Mix all marinade ingredients and pour over chicken.

3. Refrigerate them for at least two hours.

4. Preheat oven to 380 F.

5. Place the chicken onto a large baking dish, and cover with foil.

6. Bake for about 30 minutes.

7. Remove foil and bake for a further 10 to 15 minutes.

8. Serve warm.

23. Smoked BBQ Chicken Wings

Servings: 4

Preparation Time: 2 hours and 10 minutes

Nutrition Facts: Serving size: 1/4 of a recipe (8 ounces)

Percent daily values based on the Reference Daily Intake (RDI) for a 2000 calorie diet.

(Calories 421, Total Fat 42, Total Carbohydrates 10g, Sugar 2g Protein 31g)

Ingredients

4 lbs. chicken wings

2/3 cup of BBQ rub (any)

1/2 cup of vegetable oil

1 cup of BBQ sauce

Instructions

1. Preheat your smoker to 250 F.

2. Brush the wings generously with oil.

3. Coat the chicken wings with the BBQ rub and place in your smoker.

4. Cook for about 2 hours.

5. Remove the chicken onto the serving plate.

6. Brush with BBQ sauce and serve immediately.

24. Japanese Spicy Chicken Wings

Servings: 4　　　　**Preparation Time:** about 1 hour and 10 minutes

Nutrition Facts:　　Serving size: 1/4 of a recipe (8 ounces)

Percent daily values based on the Reference Daily Intake (RDI) for a 2000 calorie diet.

(Calories 488, Total Fat 23, Total Carbohydrates 16g, Sugar 12g Protein 30g)

Ingredients

3 lbs. chicken wings　　　　1/2 tsp ground red pepper

1/2 tsp ground black pepper　　Salt to taste

1/4 cup of brown sugar

4 Tbsp soy sauce

2 cloves garlic minced

1 Tbsp fresh grated ginger

1 Tbsp balsamic vinegar

Vegetable oil for frying

2 Tbsp sesame seeds

Instructions

1. Place the chicken wings onto a baking sheet; season with peppers and salt and refrigerate.

2. Heat all remaining ingredients (except oil and sesame) in a saucepan over medium heat.

3. Stir and cook until boil.

4. Remove from the heat and let it cool down.

5. Heat oil in a large heavy-bottomed skillet over medium-high heat.

6. Fry the chicken wings for about 5 minutes per side (recommended fry in batches).

7. Transfer your fried chicken wings directly to the sauce and toss to coat well.

8. Sprinkle with sesame seeds and serve.

25. Air Fryer Chicken Wings in Tamari Marinade

Servings: 4   **Preparation Time:** 1 hour and 15 minutes

Inactive time: About 4 hours

Nutrition Facts: Serving size: 1/4 of a recipe (8 ounces)

Percent daily values based on the Reference Daily Intake (RDI) for a 2000 calorie diet.

(Calories 426, Total Fat 42, Total Carbohydrates 15g, Sugar 14g Protein 44g)

Ingredients

20 chicken wings

Marinade

2 garlic cloves minced   1/3 cup of fresh lemon juice

1 cup of tamari sauce

1 Tbsp mustard

2 Tbsp fresh ginger, grated

1/3 cup of sesame oil (avocado or canola)

Instructions

1. Place the chicken wings in a large container (or divide them into two).

2. Mix all ingredients for marinade; stir to combine well.

3. Pour the mixture over the chicken and toss to coat.

4. Refrigerate for at least four hours.

5. Set air fryer to 400 F.

6. Cook your chicken in two batches.

7. Cook for 12 to 13 minutes.

8. Remove the air fryer tray, flip the wings, and cook for a further 12 to 13 minutes.

9. If you want well-done chicken, you can increase heat to 420 F and bake for additional 5 minutes.

10. Repeat the process with another batch.

11. Serve warm.

26. Lemon Pepper Wings in Crockpot

Servings: 4

Preparation Time: about 6 hours

Nutrition Facts

Serving size: 1/4 of a recipe (8 ounces)

Percent daily values based on the Reference Daily Intake (RDI) for a 2000 calorie diet.

(Calories 522, Total Fat 44, Total Carbohydrates 14g, Sugar 12g Protein 27g)

Ingredients

18 chicken wings

Salt and pepper to taste

3 Tbsp Lemon Pepper seasoning

1 1/2 cups of chicken broth

2 Tbsp fresh lemon juice

1 Tbsp lemon rind

Instructions

1. Season the chicken with salt and pepper.

2. Place the chicken into a Crockpot.

3. Mix all remaining ingredients in a bowl.

4. Pour the mixture over the chicken.

5. Cover and cook on LOW setting for 5 to 6 hours.

6. Serve warm.

27. Crispy Breaded Chicken Wings

Servings: 4

Preparation Time: 50 to 55 minutes

Inactive time: About two hours

Nutrition Facts: Serving size: 1/4 of a recipe (8 ounces)

Percent daily values based on the Reference Daily Intake (RDI) for a 2000 calorie diet.

(Calories 509, Total Fat 34, Total Carbohydrates 14g, Sugar 12g Protein 22g)

Ingredients

4 lbs. chicken wings, cleaned and drained

4 Tbsp hot rub powder for chicken

1/4 cup of olive oil

1 Tbsp honey

1 Tbsp corn flour

1 cup of flour for all-purpose

Vegetable or seed oil for frying

Salt and ground pepper to taste

Instructions

1. Season the chicken wings with salt and pepper; place in a large container.

2. Rub the chicken with oil.

3. Mix the rub powder, remaining oil, and honey; rub your chicken generously.

4. Cover and refrigerate for at least two hours.

5. Mix the corn flour, all-purpose flour, and salt and pepper in a deep dish.

6. Heat the oil in a large saucepan (or deep fryer) to 375 F.

7. Remove the chicken from the fridge and roll each wing in a flour mixture.

8. Fry the chicken until golden brown or until internal temperature reaches 165 F.

9. Serve hot.

28. Mexican Hot Chicken Wings

Servings: 4

Preparation Time: about 55 minutes

Inactive time: About two hours

Nutrition Facts: Serving size: 1/4 of a recipe (8 ounces)

Percent daily values based on the Reference Daily Intake (RDI) for a 2000 calorie diet.

(Calories 522, Total Fat 44, Total Carbohydrates 14g, Sugar 12g Protein 27g)

Ingredients

4 lbs. chicken wings

1/2 cup of hot sauce

1/4 tsp curry

1/4 tsp fresh thyme

1 Tbsp garlic minced

1 tsp jalapeño pepper finely chopped

1 tsp hot paprika (crushed)

2 Tbsp fresh lemon juice

Salt to taste

Oil for frying

Instructions

1. Place the chicken wings in a large container or divide them into two.

2. Mix all ingredients in a bowl (except oil) and pour over the chicken; toss to coat well.

3. Refrigerate for at least two hours.

4. Heat the oil in a large saucepan (or deep fryer) to 375 F.

5. Fry the chicken in batches until golden brown or until internal temperature reaches 165 F.

6. Serve hot with salad or your favorite dressing.

29. Chicken Wings with Darker Maple Syrup Glaze

Servings: 4

Preparation Time: about 55 minutes

Nutrition Facts:

Serving size: 1/4 of a recipe (8 ounces)

Percent daily values based on the Reference Daily Intake (RDI) for a 2000 calorie diet.

(Calories 289, Total Fat 24, Total Carbohydrates 7g, Sugar 5g Protein 28g)

Ingredients

20 chicken wings

1/3 cup of melted butter

4 Tbsp Darker maple syrup

2 Tbsp mustard (any)

2 Tbsp soy or tamari sauce

2 Tbsp balsamic vinegar

1/4 tsp red pepper flakes

Salt and ground pepper to

taste

Instructions

1. Preheat oven to 400 F.

2. Place the chicken wings in a large container.

3. Mix all remaining ingredients in a bowl; stir well.

4. Pour the mixture over the chicken and toss to coat well.

5. Arrange your chicken wings onto a baking sheet lined with foil.

6. Bake for about 50 to 55 minutes.

7. Serve warm.

30. Buffalo Wild Hot Sauce Wings

Servings: 4 **Preparation Time:** about 1 hour and 10 minutes

Nutrition Facts: Serving size: 1/4 of a recipe (8 ounces)

Percent daily values based on the Reference Daily Intake (RDI) for a 2000 calorie diet.

(Calories 498, Total Fat 23, Total Carbohydrates 5g, Sugar 5g Protein 32g)

Ingredients

3 lbs. chicken wings

4 Tbsp vegetable oil

Salt and ground red pepper to taste

1 tsp garlic powder

1 tsp onion powder

Sauce

1/2 cup of hot sauce

1 Tbsp red chili paste

4 Tbsp melted butter

2 Tbsp strained honey

Instructions

1. Preheat oven to 400 F.

2. Rub the chicken wings with oil.

3. Mix the salt, pepper, garlic, and onion powder, and rub the chicken generously.

4. Arrange the chicken onto the rack place it on a baking sheet.

5. Bake for about 55 to 60 minutes. (flip the wings two to three times halfway through)

6. Heat the hot sauce, chili paste, butter, and honey.

7. Bring to boil and stir for one minute.

8. Remove the chicken from the oven and brush generously with the hot sauce mixture.

9. Return the chicken to the oven and broil it for two to three minutes until sauce caramelized.

10. Serve immediately.

Summary

As we said at the beginning of this book, no matter how you prepare the chicken wings, you will not go wrong. They are so tasty, juicy, or crispy, fulfilling and satisfying. Chicken wings can be a delicious snack, dinner, or lunch great for game days and barbecues.

Your cooked chicken wings can be stored in a refrigerator for up to four days. We recommend use of a sealable container to store the wings and when you put them in the refrigerator, leave the lid off until the temperature has cooled to below 40 F. Then seal with a lid and eat within the four days.

If you eat chicken wings 2 times a week, you fill your body with nutrients and vitamins.

Good appetite!!

Sources:

- https://www.nationalchickencouncil.org/chicken-wing-history/
- https://www.therecipe.com/chicken-wing-sauces-ranked/
- https://wingsquad.com/wing-squad-delivers-most-popular-chicken-wings-flavors/
- https://www.grillcookbake.com/outdoor-cooking/chicken-wing-survey/
- https://www.euro-poultry.com/blog/6-unique-wings-products-that-will-impress-your-guests
- https://foodsided.com/2020/01/23/why-are-chicken-wings-and-football-the-ultimate-winning-combination/

Congrats! Note from the Wizard Chef

You've reached the end of the book!

Thank you for finishing Best Chicken Wing Ideas: Quick Chicken Wing Recipes, Best Hot Wings Recipe, Fried Chicken And A Complete Cookbook Of Wing Ideas!

If so, would you mind taking 30 seconds to leave a quick review on Amazon? We worked hard to bring you books that you enjoy! Plus, it helps authors like us produce more books like this in the future!

Here's where to go to leave a review now:

=> *http://successwithnow.com/best-chicken-wings*

Customer reviews

★★★★★ 4.8 out of 5

399 global ratings

Stars	Percentage
5 star	88%
4 star	9%
3 star	2%
2 star	1%
1 star	1%

˅ How are ratings calculated?

Review this product

Share your thoughts with other customers

[Write a customer review]

Printed in Great Britain
by Amazon